BLAME IT ON THE UNTZ

First published in India by HarperCollins *Children's Books* 2025
An imprint of HarperCollins *Publishers*

HarperCollins Publishers India, Cyber City, Building 10-A,
Gurugram, Haryana-122002, India

www.harpercollins.co.in

2 4 6 8 10 9 7 5 3 1

P-ISBN: 978-93-6989-123-8
E-ISBN: 978-93-6989-269-3

Series design by Denise Antao
Layout and design in Quicksand 10pt/16 by Isha Nagar

Printed and bound at Thomson Press India Ltd

*

HarperCollins Publishers, Macken House, 39/40 Mayor Street Upper,
Dublin 1, D01 C9W8, Ireland

This book is produced from independently certified FSC® paper to ensure responsible forest management.

BLAME IT ON THE UNTZ

WRITTEN AND
ILLUSTRATED BY
LAVANYA KARTHIK

HCCB
HARPERCOLLINS
CHILDREN'S BOOKS

For Ashwini, the Untz my heart beats—and burps—to

CHAPTER 1
Spelling Trouble with an H

I stared at the list pinned to the noticeboard.

Were my eyes playing tricks on me?

I moved closer and stared again.

Oh no!

Was Miss Meher playing tricks on me?

Behind me, the rest of Class 5C jostled and elbowed each other for a better view.

'Move, ya, Adi,' Phani whined. 'Trying to hypnotize

the list or what?'

'This is not possible,' I spluttered. 'This can't be happening.'

'Huh?'

'This is not possible. This can't be happening.'

'Wuh?'

'This is . . . '

'I think the board has hypnotized Adi,' Kumail sniggered. 'Now he thinks he is a parrot.'

My left eye had begun to twitch. My knees were shaking like jelly, the real deal; not the kind my grandfather makes that sets like cement and once caused Papa to chip a tooth.

'A parrot about to explode,' Miriam said, peering into my face. 'Eh, what happened, ya, Adi?''

'I'm . . . I . . . I've been put in a group for the Grade 5 Music Gala.'

'Everyone has been put into a group,' Kumail said, shrugging. 'So what?''

'A group!' I hissed, like that giant snake living in the Hogwarts toilets.

Kumail peered at the list. Then he gurgled with laughter like a choked drain. 'Oi, Adi, you have Angry and Chinmay!' I turned around to glare at him, which only made him gurgle harder.

'And . . . HAHAHA!'

I closed my eyes and waited for the final blow.
' . . . and Faizal!'

'Ya, so what?' I snapped.

Kumail said nothing. Instead, everyone turned and looked across the classroom where a head like a lollipop, topped with a frizzy mop of hair, grinned at me. Just to be clear, it wasn't a head perched by itself on a table or something. It was attached to two arms, two legs and about two trillion tonnes of Annoying, all packaged into a creature formerly called Risha. I'll explain why 'formerly' in a minute.

I narrowed my eyes and turned back to the list. Aha! No wonder! She was in a group with Mary, Chinci and Junaid, all of whom played instruments and won stuff. That's the group I should have been in, I thought. Well, minus the lollipop. She could have Angry and Chinmay and Faizal. But of course, I couldn't ask without making her crow in joy. 'You're going down, Adi,' the annoying creature formerly known as Risha Popli sniffed. Every few months, her mother sent the school a letter announcing that Risha's name was now to be spelt with two Hs, or four Rs, or three rhinoceroses or whatever, because a world-famous astrologer said this was necessary to ward off the evil eye. Apparently, evil eyes can be distracted by weird spellings. If my parents were to show up in school asking that my name be spelled with four Qs and a radish, Principal Vichare would have sent them straight back home, and me with them. But Risha's mother was a famous journalist and on the school board and, it must be said, very scary, so her daughter's name was now Class 5C's personal Spelling Bee.

If you asked me, the fastest way to ward off the evil eye—or even a whole army of them—would be to simply lock them in a room with Risha. Two minutes with her, and they would be sobbing and screaming for their mummies. But since no one had, in fact, asked me, Class 5C of Sunny Valley High School now had a pinboard near the door, announcing the most recent spelling of her name. Today, it read

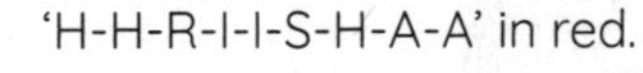
'H-H-R-I-I-S-H-A-A' in red.

'I am not,' I told Hhriishaa. 'Also, they've spelled your name wrong.'

'What? Where?' She whooshed across the room to glare at the board. 'What rubbish! It's correct only.'

'There are two Ns in "ANNOYING",' I said. 'And definitely no "H"s.'

'Oh haha, very funny!' Hhriishaa hissed. 'Let's see who laughs after the gala.'

I flinched. For as long as I had known her—which was way, way too long if you ask me (but again, no one ever does)—haha-Hhriishaa and I had been fighting for the same prizes. Second grade topper: I won. First prize in the Grade 3 spelling bee: she beat me by a point. She would, with all the extra practice with her name. Grade 4, we tied for first prize, which I still think was engineered just to keep Mrs Popli from thundering into the principal's office. Environment day essay competition, reading challenge, science quiz—everything was now a battle with the human Spelling Bee. Not that I would let her know this for a second.

'Probably me, because of how you play the bongo.'

'Ya, hahaha, as if!' Hhriishaa snapped.

'And it's a banjo, okay. The only prize your group is getting is the Weirdo prize!'

'At least my name doesn't need its own Spelling Bee,' I snapped back.

'Well, if it did, I would still win!' she said triumphantly and stomped straight back to her seat.

I ignored the giggles and whispers around me. I tried to look cool and collected and unbothered. I adjusted my face into a slight smile of supreme coolness and collectedness and unbotheredness and looked back at . . .

'Eh, Adi, you look funny.' Kumail peered into my face. 'Want to go to the little boys' room or what?'

CHAPTER 2
Crocodiles, Boxes and Burps

'Miss, there's been a mistake!' I said, as soon as Miss Meher walked in.

She sighed, and muttered, 'I knew it.' She dropped an enormous pile of our notebooks onto the table. 'Everybody in your seats, please,' she said. 'Grammar books out!'

'Miss,' I said again. 'I shouldn't be in a group. I won the medal at last year's gala for best performance. And the year before that, and . . . '

'Miss, Adi's showing off,' someone whined. Someone with a head like a lollipop, and two radishes in her name.
I gulped. Behind me, I could hear the class sniggering

and whispering words like 'always complaining' and 'such a nerd'.

'Miss,' I said again. 'Please, can I just play solo?'

Miss Meher shook her head. 'No solos this year, Adi,' she said. 'Principal Vichare wants everyone to participate. Learn to work in teams. Only groups this year.'

'Then Miss, can I not take part?'

'Miss, he's just afraid he'll lose,' someone shouted. No prizes for guessing who.

I turned around to glare at her but she was too busy hiccupping with laughter.

'Then, Miss, can I be in a different group?'

The sniggers behind me grew a little louder.

'The groups are final, Adi,' she replied. 'No changes. This year we are going to learn to work together. Not worry about winning and losing.'

'I could be my own group, Miss.'

'No.'

'Please, Miss!'

Miss Meher sighed again. Then she looked up at the class.

'Would anyone like to switch places with Adi?' she asked.

I turned around and smiled. Listen, I was really good. I practised for hours. My classmates knew it.

A sea of faces stared back at me. Some frowned, some grinned, some made weird faces and clutched their heads in horror (okay, that was mostly that pest, Risha). Absolutely none of them did what they should have, which was jump up and say, 'Miss, Adi's brilliant at the keyboard! We want him!'

I suddenly felt like one of those wildebeest crossing a river on the National Geographic channel Papa likes watching, while a bunch of hungry crocodiles lurk in the water, waiting to . . .

GULP!

I bet you think I'm just fussing about all this. What's the big deal about group work anyway?

Remember that crocodile lurking in the water while you, innocent wildebeest, stand on the banks, quivering with fear? Well, take that crocodile, make it ten times larger with a hundred times more teeth . . . then imagine the crocodile that would eat HIM! That beast . . . now that's group work.

Those teeth . . . that's all the different opinions you have to listen to, when all they need to do is listen to YOU.

Those claws . . . That's the extra work you have to do because the rest of the group will just waste time, fool around and totally forget to do their part.

That tail . . . that is the tail of bad grades that will smack you off your feet, and send you flying.

Those jaws . . . . the terrible jaws of helpless frustration, chewing and chewing you until . . .

'Your face is all funny. And why are you chewing like that?'

I looked up from the music notation book I was staring at, eating one of the cheese parathas Malti Aunty had packed for me. It was lunch break, and I was at my desk as usual, enjoying the peace and quiet while the rest of the class ran around like screaming monkeys in the playground. Until now, anyway.

'What do you want?' I asked, scowling up at Angira Kamath. I didn't have to look very far, though. Angry, as everyone called her, because she looked like an angry bird, was also about the same size as one.

'I want you to be in a different group too,' she frowned. 'Such a showoff you are.'

Oh, right. I had been so focused on getting out of a group, I hadn't paid attention to the one I was in. The one Haahoo-hriishaa had said would get the Weirdo prize.

'Listen, I can play the . . .'

'Ya, we know. You won't stop reminding us!' she snapped. Then she sniffed the air and frowned even harder. 'Ugh, cheese,' she said. 'I hate cheese.'

'What's that?' Angry poked at the little foil-covered box Dadu had tucked into my lunch bag.

'Jelly,' I said. 'My grandfather makes it himself. Want some?'

'I hate jelly!'

A large shadow fell across the desk. I turned around... and jumped. Chinmay had silently appeared beside my desk. He was at least a foot taller than the rest of fifth grade, and probably half of sixth grade too, and very quiet. Our PE teacher was always begging him to try out for the basketball team. But Chinmay seemed to prefer hanging out by himself at break time.

We stared at each other in silence.

Finally, I asked, 'So do you play any instruments?'

Chinmay continued to stare at me.

Angry said, 'Ya. Flute.' Then she hissed, 'I hate the flute.'
And now a fourth kid slouched up and joined the group. His shirt was untucked, his shoes were covered in the red mud from the playground and his hair stuck out in a hundred different directions. He slid across the floor and came to a neat stop beside Angry.

'Faizal in da house,' he announced, making strange

waggles with his fingers.

I sighed.

'Bro,' he said. 'We're so going to win the gala.'

I sat up. Of course, Faizal knew just how well I played.

'Yeah, right,' Angry said.

'No, seriously, bro,' he said. 'Listen.'

His hands flew to his lips.

'Untz! Untz! Untz!'

He looked up at us, probably expecting applause.

No one moved.

He went back to making more weird noises. Groans and clicks, whines and hiccups. Jingles, jangles, sneezes, wheezes.

'Toobytoobytoobytooby! Phat! Phatta phat! Dishhhh!'

Faizal raised his arms up like he was showering us with blessings. Or maybe his shirt was really sweaty. 'Ladies and gentlemen, boys and girl, did you feel the Untz?'

'The who-ntz?'

'The Untz! The beat! The rhythm!' And he made that noise again. 'UNTZ! UNTZ! UNTZ! UNTZ! DAKKA DIKKA DAKKA DIKKA UNTZ UNTZ UNTZ!'

'Sounds like dishes falling down the stairs,' I said.

'And like you fell after them,' said Angry.

'Bro, it's beatboxing! It's, like, totally cool.'

'I hate boxes,' Angry said. 'And I am not making those noises in front of the school.'

'You don't have to, bro,' said Faizal. 'I'll make the beats, you play the flute, Chinmay can play the tambourine and Adi—'

'We know what Adi does.' Angry rolled her eyes.

'I play sonatas, okay!' I stood up, glaring right back at her.

'Who-natas?"

‘Sonatas! Classical music! There is no burping or boxing in a sonata!’

‘Beatbox, bro, beatbox.’

‘You want me to play a sonata while you burp and hiccup and throw dishes down the stairs?”

‘Chill, bro,’ Faizal drawled. ‘Feel the Untz!’

Chill! Chill!! Seriously? I felt those crocodiles rear up at me out of the water. Well, as if! I wasn’t just another wildebeest. I wasn’t going to just wade in and be chomped. I—

‘Cool, you’re dancing, bro,’ Faizal said, watching my feet splash through imaginary water. ‘Maybe you can break while I beatbox.’

‘I’m . . . I’m not dancing! And don’t tell me to chill. We can’t be beating boxes in the gala. We just can’t!’

But the three of them just ignored me and started chattering amongst themselves.

I saw my medal vanishing down a crocodile’s grinning mouth . . . GULP!

CHAPTER 3
Deafeningly a Plan

'This is a disaster!' I looked up into an assortment of faces peering at me from around the dining table. Nice. I had been mumbling to myself again.

'It's your favourite potato curry,' Mummy said, frowning.

'And it's delicious.' She popped a big lump of greasy vegetable into her mouth as proof.

'Should I make you some jelly later?' Dadu offered.

'Get some on Swiggy,' Papa said. 'I beg you.'

'No jelly!' I said. 'And I don't mean the food. I am battling a crocodile at the Music Gala.'

'Try playing a song instead,' Papa joked.

I sighed. Papa didn't understand about the crocodiles. He thought school was all fun and games and jolly classmates. Maybe it *had* been back when he was my age and dinosaurs grazed in the school compound. But there was a reason dinosaurs went extinct, and crocodiles still lurked in gurgling river beds, waiting to snap talented keyboard-playing boys in their gigantic jaws and just crunch and munch and . . .

'Why is he chewing on the air like that?' Malti Aunty, our cook and resident giver of advice no one ever asks for, bustled out of the kitchen with a big stack of chapatis. 'Here, eat a chapati, son. Eat ten! You're so thin your ears are bigger than your head!' Mummy and Papa nodded sadly. They had taken to nodding sadly every time Malti Aunty made a silly comment like this. Lately, they'd even begun refusing to sign me up for after-school classes, saying I needed to 'be a child'.

'Maybe you could write to the principal and say I cannot be in a group,' I suggested.

'Oh. And what reason could I give?' Mummy asked.

'Erm, the evil eye?" I suggested.

'Nice try,' Mummy said. 'He'd probably tell us to just spell your name differently.'

'Please!' I whined. 'Groups are crocodiles! You know how much I hate them!'

'Absolutely not!'

'Pleeeeeeaaase!'

'Listen, Adi,' she said, with a glint in her eye. 'Remember that advanced maths class you wanted me to sign you up for?'

'You mean the one you refused to send me to?'

'The very same,' Mummy said. 'So, I am willing to sign you up.'

'Yaaaay!'

'But only if you stay in your group for the gala. I am absolutely, definitely not going to let you pull out of it.'

'Deafeningly!' My brother Sunny, who was five and loved big words, waved his spoon in the air.

'Definitely, Sunny,' I said. 'Not deafeningly.'

‘Absolutelimentally!’ he replied.

‘Didn’t you win a prize at the gala last year?” Dadu asked. ‘I remember I made you my special mango pudding to celebrate.’

‘We all remember that day,’ Papa said, rubbing his jaw.

Dadu rolled his eyes, mumbled something about people with weak jaws and went back to his food.

‘Adi, just remember, don’t practise all day,’ Mummy said.

‘You need to go out and play also, all right? Be with your friends.’

‘He has friends?’ Malti Aunty, like a bad cold, was back, tossing salad onto everyone’s plates.

‘Where is that boy you used to play with? Fuzzy, was it?’ Dadu asked. ‘You used to be inseparable.’

I popped a big chunk of shredded cabbage into my mouth so I didn’t have to reply.

‘Insoupable,’ Sunny said, lighting up at this brand-new addition to his word collection. ‘Adi is insoupable.’

Later, in the peace and quiet of my room, I considered my options.

Maybe I could pretend to fall sick and drop out? But the gala was six weeks away! I would have to stay sick for a very long time and I didn't think Mummy or Papa or our resident Sherlock Holmes, Malti Aunty, would let me. Besides, I liked school!

I could fall 'sick' the day before the gala. But that would still mean six weeks of practice and being part of a group. And I could just see that Heyho-Hhrishaa scurrying around, telling everyone I did it on purpose!

Crocodiles, I thought. Everywhere I looked. I would just have to make sure I wasn't chomped.

CHAPTER 4

A Comb for the Crocodile

There was no mention of the gala for the next two days at school, which suited me just fine. It made it easier to steer clear of Angry and Faizal and Chinmay. To be honest, they seemed to be steering clear of me too.

Then on Friday, right after long break, Miss Meher set more crocodiles loose.

She made us all get up from our places and sit with our group members. I waited at my desk, since I was in the front row. Then I turned and saw that Angry and Faizal had gone to sit beside Chinmay. Huh, they could have called me, I thought, before getting up and wriggling and pushing and tripping through the crush of boys and girls to the very back of the class. I sat down in the empty seat beside Angry, who very pointedly shifted away.

'Groups,' Miss Meher said once everyone had finished squealing, dragging chairs and falling over each other. 'I want you to all to come up with a song you can perform. Not more than five minutes long, as we have groups from all three sections of Grade 5. I expect you to discuss what each of you can do—sing or play an instrument. This will be a group effort, so everyone has to contribute.'

Everyone in class started talking at once. Everyone, that is, except the four of us. We sat there silently, looking everywhere but at each other. Miss Meher looked around the class, then frowned when she caught sight of us.

This is stupid, I thought. I obviously needed to take charge.

Taking a deep breath, I turned and said, 'Listen.'

'No.' Angry crossed her arms. 'I hate listening.'

'I haven't even said anything yet.'

'Let me guess,' she said. 'Your idea is that you will play your tomatoes and we will clap our hands or something.'
I could feel my face turn red as a tomato.

'No, of course not,' I lied. 'What rubbish. Also, it's sonatas, okay? Not tomatoes. Anyway, what can you play on your flute?'

'Doe a deer, a female deer,' she said. 'I hate deer.'

'And?'

'That's it, doe a deer, a female deer.'

That wasn't bad, I thought. 'Cool,' I said. 'I can play that song too.'

'Not the song,' she said. 'I can play "Doe a deer a female deer".'

'That's one line, Angry,' I said.

'That's what I can play,' she said.

'One line?'

'Yes.'

'Seriously?'

'YES!' Angry glared.

'Chinmay, you?' I asked.

Chinmay turned his head slowly towards me. Then he

reached into his pocket and pulled out a plastic comb and a piece of paper.

'You want to comb your hair now?' I asked.

Chinmay shook his head. Then, he placed the paper over the teeth of the comb, put it to his lips and began to make noises like an angry bee.

'So cool, bro,' Faizal breathed.

It really wasn't.

'Can you play Doe a deer?' Angry asked.

Chinmay promptly treated us to the angry bee version of the song.

I looked across the class at Hhriishaa. Her group were high-fiving each other and grinning like monkeys. Junaid had drawn up a list of songs they could all play. Maria and Chinci were arm in arm, doing some sort of jig. I glared

at Risha. I could just see that medal in the water, being snatched up in a hungry crocodile's jaws, gobbled up and chewed up and then . . .

'Hungry or what, Adi?' Kumail asked, leaning back over his chair. 'Didn't eat your tiffin?'

'Look,' I said to the group. 'Don't you want to win the medal?'

'I hate medals,' Angry said.

'Bro, who cares,' Faizal said.

'So we'll just prove everyone right, then,' I sighed.

'Right about what?'

'About being weirdos. About us winning the weirdo prize.'

'Who said that?' Angry's eyes blazed. 'Was it that Kumail? I'll fix him.'

'No, no,' I said hurriedly. 'Not Kumail. And I'm not going to snitch, okay? But . . . that's what they are saying.'

Listen, I wasn't lying, was I? Someone did say those words to me.

I sneaked another peek at Hhrishaaisha's group. Now all

four had linked their arms and were hopping from left to right and giggling.

'They're probably gossiping about us right now,' I added. Faizal and Angry looked at each other. Chinmay looked at me.

'Children.' Miss Meher clapped her hands. 'All of you, settle down. Let's hear your ideas.'

***

'Park?' My mother sounded confused. 'You're going to the park?'

It was Saturday afternoon, and I was trying to slide my shoes on.

'I don't understand,' Mummy said, setting her laptop down.

'I have to go meet my group,' I said again. 'In the park.'

'Who are you,' Papa huffed, lying on his back on a yoga mat in the living room. 'And what have you done to our Adi?'

'Miss Meher said all the groups had to meet on the weekend and get to know each other better.' It turned out that only Hhriishaa's group had everything figured out including, I bet, the thank you speech they would give when the medal was placed in their sweaty, grabby hands. The rest of the class was just like our group, moody and irritable and full of people thinking combs and shoeboxes and their best friend's left ear were actual musical instruments.

'I want to come,' Sunny said, jumping around me in excitement.

'It's for classwork, Sunny,' I said. 'Not to play.'

'I can do glasswork,' Sunny said.

'But . . . but . . . you never go to the park!' Mummy was still struggling with what I'd told her. 'Even when we beg you.'

'I so go . . . have gone to the park!'

'The last time you set foot in the park was when you were eight,' Dadu announced. 'After that, you refused. Or burst into tears. Even when I promised to bake you brownies.'

'That might have been because of the brownies,' Papa muttered.

'I want to do glasswork,' Sunny announced, slipping on his shoes.

'I didn't burst into tears, Dadu!' I huffed. 'I was doing my maths homework. Then I had tuition. Then I . . . '

'You spend more time studying and going to tuition than any ten-year-old I know!' Dadu thundered.

'I am the only ten-year-old you know,' I reminded him.

'Glasswork!' Sunny yelled.

'Come on, Sunny,' I said and ran for the door.

CHAPTER 5
A Meeting in the Park

The big municipal park down the road from my apartment complex turned out to be the most convenient place for everyone to meet. No music talk, Miss Meher had said, as if we were in danger of bursting into song beside the yoga corner and scaring away the senior citizens laughter club. Only bonding. Getting to know one another. Becoming a team.

I wandered down the jogging track, past the sand pit with those special swings for babies that parents seem to love, but babies never do. Sunny hopped and skipped beside me, a big smile on his face. We watched a bunch of tinies scrambling up the climbing frame while their moms and dads stood around looking at their phones, and looking up occasionally to shout something utterly pointless, like 'Rehaan, climb nicely, beta' or 'Tia! Don't fall!' I'd been one of those tinies myself, though Dadu was more the sort to shout, 'Whoever gets to the top first gets a box of special homemade jelly.'

'You're mumbling and chewing . . . again.' I looked up at the branch above. A pair of very dirty shoes was hanging inches from my nose. Attached to the shoes was an equally dusty pair of jeans, a T-shirt with a laughing horse on it and, at last, a face with a familiar frown.

'Hi Angry,' I said. 'You're early.'

'So are you.' Angry dropped down from the tree branch. 'Also, I hate being late. Who's this?'

'Glasswork,' Sunny explained.

'Good for you,' she replied.

We wandered down the path to the old bandstand by the pond. We stood by the railing, peering into the brown water below. I sighed. I could have been home all this time, practising one of my medal-winning songs. Yet, here I was, gazing into a puddle of murky brown goo, while . . .

'Hi, Faizal. Hi Chinmay,' Angry said.

I looked up to see the rest of the team walking towards us. Well, one of them was. Faizal jerked and twitched and finger-waggled to a tune only he could hear. His lips were keeping time to the tune too, with a series of smacks, burps and whistles.

'CHAKA-OOOH!' he finished with a flourish, then stuck a fist in the air. Angry promptly gave him a fist bump.

Then he grinned and stuck his hand out to Sunny. 'Yo, dude!' he said, bumping fists with my little brother. 'Remember me?'

'Deafeningly!' Sunny

squealed. I was pretty sure he didn't.

'Yo, bro,' Faizal turned to me, his fist hovering inches from my face.

I stared at it until Angry sighed, raised my wrist and bumped it against Faizal's.

We stood there in silence, looking at each other. Birds chirped, squirrels chittered, people squawked. Cars honked in the distance. The faint echo of 'Rehaan, don't get hurt' wafted in the breeze.

I took a deep breath. 'Okay, so for the gala, I was thinking—'

'Ha!' Angry smirked. 'I knew you would crack first. Miss Meher said no music talk.'

'Ya, but we need to practise and be ready for it.'

'Miss Meher SAID!'

We stood around in silence again. More birds, more people, more honks. Rehaan was now being told to run carefully and not fall. Faizal grinned and began bobbing his head.

'You hear that?' he asked, his head bobbing.

'Hear what?'

'Rehaan, don't fall,' he said, in a sing-song way.

'Huh?'

'Rehaan, don't fall!' Faizal snapped his fingers.

'Again, huh?'

'Rehaan, don't fall, Rehaan, don't fall,' Faizal started singing. Now his feet kept tune with his fingers.

'People are watching us,' I hissed. 'Faizal, stop it,'

'Who is RE-haan? Who IS Reh-AAN?' Faizal sang. Chinmay, Angry and I stood there, staring at him.

And now his hands flew up to his face.

A series of clicks and hoots and burps followed.

'DAB CHIK DAB WHO IS REHAAN?' Faizal sang.

Sunny started clapping in time to Faizal's singing. Then, as if our little group weren't embarrassing enough, he started dancing around Faizal.

'Is he okay?' An elderly lady stopped beside us. 'Does he need a doctor?'

‘I think the rest of us do,’ I muttered.

Faizal ticked and tocked, clicked and squeaked, hiccupped and whooshed.

With a final flourish and a ‘DAB CHIK KAPOW!’, Faizal finally stopped.

‘Did you feel that?’ He flashed a toothy smile.

‘Strange? Weird? Embarrassed? Yes, yes we did,’ I said.

‘The Untz, bro!’ Faizal said. ‘Did you feel the Untz?’

‘I did! I did!’ Sunny squealed. I watched as Faizal gave him a high five and a fist bump.

I blinked. Chinmay looked puzzled; his eyebrows had dipped towards each other, like two furry caterpillars holding hands. Angry looked, well, angry.

Faizal beamed at us. 'The Untz, ya. The beat. You know—' His hands flew up to his face again. A series of strange noises followed. 'Untz! Untz! Untz!'

'I feel it!' Sunny squealed, bouncing around us. 'Deafeningly!'

'Faizal,' I said, as if I was talking to a small child. 'It's really interesting and all, but we can't play this . . . erm, noise, at the Gala.'

'Why not?'

'Because this will not win a medal,' I said.

'Who cares?' he said. 'Bro, you need to chill.'

'Chill?' I felt my face go hot and red.

'Ya, bro. Just, like, chillax.'

'Chillax!' I sputtered.

'Chill!' Sunny gurgled. 'Chillax, bro. Chillax your chill!'

'Ooh, good one, Sunny!' Faizal nodded.

I watched them high-five again.

'Hey, Chinmay! What happened?' Angry called.

Chinmay was looking out towards the main road, as if he was listening very carefully to something. He tapped his ear, pointed in the direction he'd been looking, and frowned.

'I can't hear anything,' Faizal said. 'Only buses . . . oh, and a cat? Hey, where are you going?'

CHAPTER 6
Enter Danger Cat!

'Where is he going?' I panted, struggling to keep pace with Angry and Faizal. We were all trying to keep up with Chinmay, who was moving faster than I'd ever seen him move before.

We followed Chinmay all the way through the park, out of the big iron gates, and onto the road. It wasn't very busy that time of the afternoon, but I still reached down and gripped Sunny's hand firmly in mine.

'Watch out!' I yelled, as Chinmay bounded onto the road. Faizal ran with him, straight for the cat.

'Oh! There!' Angry gasped. Right in the middle of the road

stood a very large, very bushy cat, wailing louder than I'd ever heard a cat yowl. And hurtling down the road, straight towards it, was a yellow school van. I gulped and tightened my grip on Sunny's hand.

The van honked as it drew near.

Angry yelled. Everything seemed to move very quickly.

But someone was quicker still!

With a piercing shriek, the cat launched itself off the ground, straight up into the air . . . and onto the front of the van!

There was a screech of brakes, a squeal of tyres, and a loud thunk and scream as the conductor flew across the bus and into the grillwork behind the driver's seat.

'My heart!' the driver cried, her hands pressed to her chest. 'That cat almost killed me!'

'That's the pre-primary school van!' Angry gasped. 'And that's Kanmani Aunty driving. I used to travel on that van when I was in nursery.'

'Me too!' I said.

'Me three!' Sunny squealed. We had all spent time in Kanmani Aunty's bus as tinies, while her younger sister, Kanaka, kept a close eye on us and made sure we always had our seatbelts on when the bus was moving. I peered in through the windows. No tinies, I noted, with relief. Just poor Kanaka Aunty, who had clearly ignored her own rules about seatbelts.

Faizal opened the van door and helped Kanaka Aunty out. 'That cat!' she groaned. 'Third time this month! He does it on purpose, I swear!' We watched as she tottered out onto the road. 'We should report it to the police, Kanmani.'

'I did,' the driver replied, wiping her forehead with a trembling hand. 'They just laughed at me.'

The cat stood in the front of the van, glaring through the windshield and hissing.

'Get off! Get off!' Kanmani Aunty waved her hands from behind the glass.

The cat hissed again and she hurriedly moved her hands away.

'RRAAARGH! GROOOOOOOOL! MIAOOOOWWWRRRRR!' I listened in awe as he made the most astonishing sounds I had ever heard anyone make. Except, possibly, Faizal.

'It's beatboxing like you, Faizal!' Angry giggled.

'Ooh!' Faizal said. 'I should join in.'

'NO!' Angry and I said in unison. Then Angry gasped. 'Chinmay, stay back! He'll scratch you.'

But Chinmay seemed utterly untouched by the cat's furious roars. He leaned in, towards the cat.

The cat froze and slowly turned towards Chinmay.

'What is Chinmay doing?' Sunny asked.

I looked closely at the way Chinmay's head moved slowly from side to side. I listened hard and, just over the sound of traffic, I realized what he was doing.

'I think he's . . . humming!'

'Son, that Danger Cat will eat you!' Kanaka Aunty called out. 'Beware!'

'Oh, I can't watch! That poor child!' Kanmani Aunty clapped her hands over her eyes.

We stood frozen, waiting for the cat to attack Chinmay. Except, he didn't.

As Chinmay hummed, the cat's eyes lost their mad gleam. His hackles subsided, his claws loosened their grip on the van, his tail gently relaxed. And, as we watched, he began to purr.

Chinmay held his hands out. We gasped as the cat leaped into Chinmay's arms and nestled against him.

'Waah!' Kanmani Aunty cried. 'A miracle!' We all broke into applause.

Sunny and I ran up to join the rest of our group by the van. Chinmay crouched down so Sunny could pet the cat. My brother gently stroked Danger Cat's back, beaming. We all stood there, grinning at each other. And for just a moment, I thought I felt . . . a hum. A buzz. Something. In the air around us. Something connecting me and Sunny and the rest of the group. Even the bus aunties and Danger Cat.

But only for a moment.

'You're blocking traffic!' a man yelled as he drove past on a scooter. Behind him sat a young man holding a goat. 'Get these cats off the road!' The goat peered down at the road as they sped past, and baaa-ed.

Cats? I looked down too. Sure enough, a small army of cats had gathered at our feet, all mewing and purring and trying to reach Chinmay.

Chinmay, still humming, carried Danger Cat back towards the park, followed by his cat army.

'He tamed that monster!' Kanmani Aunty said. 'Did you see that, Kanaka?"

'I did!' The conductor wiped a tear from her eye. 'He saved us! That evil thing would have eaten us alive today.'

'Chinmay is a superhero!' Angry said as we followed him back to the park. 'A Cat Whisperer!'

'A Cat Hummer, actually,' I said.

'And that Danger Cat throws some cool beats!' Faizal laughed. 'We should ask him to join our group for the gala!'

The gala! I had forgotten all about the song we had to choose, and the team bonding Miss Meher had asked us to do. Instead, here we were, knee-deep in cats.

'Guys,' I said. 'We need a song.'

But Faizal was crouched in the grass, patting cats and giggling at a kitten that was trying to climb up his leg. And Sunny was giggling helplessly as he lay in the grass, cats all over him. And Angry had dropped down beside him, cuddling the cats that had crawled into her lap.

'Guys?' I tried again.

Angry reached up and yanked me by the arm. I landed with a thunk beside her, rather like Kanaka Aunty from a while ago.

'Hey! Why did you . . . Oh! Shoo! Shoo!' I waved my fingers, trying to scare away the cats meowing and milling around me.

And most of them did go away except for this one white kitten. It stared at me, stared at my fingers and then with one little leap, was in my lap.

***

A row of eager faces was waiting for Sunny and me when we returned home. One look at Sunny's muddy face and Papa whisked him away for a bath. Which left me facing a barrage of questions from Mummy and Dadu. Even Malti Aunty popped out of the kitchen to gape at me.

'So?' Mummy asked, her eyes giant idlis of curiosity. 'How was it?'

'I went to the park,' I reminded her. 'Not Mars.'

'With you, it might as well have been Mars,' Malti Aunty said, pointing her rolling pin at me. 'If you're not in school or tuition, you are sitting alone in your room playing that keyboard. It's not good, I tell you.'

Why couldn't Malti Aunty go to Mars, I wondered. She could give the Martians all her advice about eating and living and how not to let their ears get bigger than their heads.

'Did you all bond, like Miss Meher told you to?' Dadu asked. 'Are you all a tight team now?'

'Erm, no. I mean, we just started. Then there was this cat, and—'

'Don't tell me about cats!' Malti Aunty shuddered. 'There is this cat over at that Popli Madam's house where I cook in the evenings. Badshah, he's called! I tell you, such a monster!'

'Who? Popli Madam?' Dadu's ears perked up at the promise of some gossip.

'No, the cat. Actually, Madam also. Always with her

horoscopes and spellings. Wanted me to add three Ms or two lemons or something to my name.' She ambled back into the kitchen, muttering about cats and the price of lemons.

***

Project Team Bonding had been hijacked by cats. All we had done was play with them, until Chinmay's mother came to pick him up in a little red car. And when the scary cat purred and wailed to be let in, she didn't say a word as Chinmay opened the door and let him hop in.

Then Angry's sister came for her, and it was just Faizal and me, watching the last of the cats wander away.

'Remember the time we climbed that tree and got stuck?' he said, pointing at one of the giant trees that dotted the park.

I did remember. We had been seven that year, and were finally allowed to go to the park alone. We had stayed up there until Dadu and Faizal's dad showed up, convinced we had been kidnapped. Instead, they had found us sitting in a tree, singing and giggling.

'I bet our parents sang a version of the "Rehaan, don't fall" song too,' I said.

'They did!' Faizal laughed. For a moment, I was worried he would break into a song or some burping again. Instead, we stood there, the silence stretching between us like over-chewed chewing gum.

'Listen, you still remember the Disco Duo?' he asked.

'No,' I lied, and then ran back home.

CHAPTER 7
Things Change

Class 5C had changed. I noticed the moment I stepped into class on Monday. Every group had met over the weekend and seemed to have instantly become besties. Boys and girls who hadn't so much as looked at each other all this while were now standing about in clumps, telling jokes and gossiping. HhrishaaYouWisha and Chinci were holding hands and singing by the water cooler. Justin, Ishan, Tenzin and Kumail already had a secret handshake and called themselves the Fundoo Four.

Was it really that easy? How come it never happened to me?

'Kumail and his group even look like each other,' Angry

observed, sliding into the empty chair beside me. She was right. They looked like they had all spent time in the boys' washroom, wetting their hair in the sink to shape it into identical spikes. At least I hope it was the sink—you could never be sure with that Kumail.

Well, they may have spikes, but we had cats. And for just a moment, I found myself smiling as I remembered the little white kitten I had played with in the park. But then I saw Hhrishaisha glance my way and whisper into Chinci's ear. I felt a cold wave of fury wash over me as they both looked at me and giggled. I suddenly felt like the cat Chinmay had rescued. I wanted to scream and leap onto the bonnet of Hhrishaa's car and scare her through the glass. And I thought about the medal I needed to win.

'You're mumbling about cats,' Angry remarked.

'That was fun!' Faizal grinned, appearing beside my desk. 'Chinmay, you are a wizard, bro.'

I swivelled around to see Chinmay at the desk to my right. 'It was amazing,' I said. 'How did you tame Danger Cat?'

Chinmay said nothing, as usual, though a tiny smile appeared on his face.

'Well, it's like your superpower, bro,' Faizal said. 'Chinmay the Superhero!' They high fived and fist bumped.

Then, things got weirder. Every group began spending even their break time huddled together, talking about the gala. We caught snatches of songs being sung or hummed in the corridor, on the field, even in the washroom. Gala fever had caught all of 5C. Well, all of 5C except the four of us. When Miss Meher asked the groups for their lists and ideas, everyone seemed to be ready. They all knew who would do what. I discovered there were plenty of keyboard players, drummers, sitarists and fiddlers in the class. But also, a lot of kids who were going to shake tambourines, swish maracas and jangle triangles. One by one, each group went up to Miss Meher's table to talk about the song they would perform.

'What about you?' Miss Meher asked, calling us to her desk. 'Tell me your ideas.'

We lined up in silence before her.

Miss Meher frowned. 'Did you figure out what instruments you could play?'

Silence again.

‘You could sing too,’ Miss Meher suggested. ‘Some groups are doing that.’

‘I hate singing,’ Angry muttered under her breath.

‘I can’t sing,’ I mumbled at the same time.

We continued to stand there, gazing at our toes.

‘Miss, Adi can play the keyboard,’ Faizal said.

Huh?

Angry stared at Faizal for a moment, then said, ‘Miss, Adi can play piñatas.’

‘Sonatas,’ I said. ‘I play sonatas.’

‘And Miss, Angry, er, Angira plays Doe a deer on the flute,’ Faizal piped up.

Miss Meher smiled and nodded. ‘What about you, Chinmay?’

Chinmay brought his comb and piece of paper out and gave Miss Meher a quick performance of Doe a deer. Miss Meher seemed startled at first, but then smiled and nodded.

And now we all looked at Faizal. I held my breath as Miss Meher asked him what he could do.

Faizal looked up at me and said, 'Miss, I can play the tambourine.'

'Wonderful, wonderful,' Miss Meher beamed. 'But how do we put all of this together into a song? Any ideas?'

The rest of my group turned to me. I thought hard. Was there a way I could combine all our different instruments into one song? Maybe mix up a few songs I knew, and figure out how to add 'Doe a deer' as a chorus?

'A medley!'

Miss Meher was delighted when I explained what we could do. 'Excellent! A perfect song for a team!'

We stared at each other. What now?

CHAPTER 8
A Miracle, a Meeting, Some Jelly

'My group is coming over this weekend,' I announced at dinner. Four pairs of idli eyes stared at me. Then it became five—Malti Aunty leaned out of the kitchen.

'Friends?' Mummy said. 'You have friends! And they are coming over!'

'They're not my friends,' I said. 'They're my group for the Music Gala. And we have to meet here because I need my keyboard.'

'It's glasswork!' Sunny announced. 'Deafeningly glasswork!'

'Friends!' Mummy squealed. 'Friends!' Then she pulled out

her phone, called her mummy and squealed, 'Adi has friends! They are coming over!'

'Friends?' I heard Nani say. 'A miracle!'

'Miracle indeed!' Malti Aunty scoffed. 'It's those extra chapatis I make you eat! Even your head is looking the right size now.'

'I'll make some jelly,' Dadu announced. 'And maybe my special brownies!'

'Please, no,' Papa said. 'We want them to stay his friends.'

***

'Are your classmates here yet?' Malti Aunty peered out of the window that Saturday, waiting to see the group. She even had her phone out, to take pictures.

'They are from fifth grade,' I reminded her. 'Not from Mars.'

'Might as well be from Mars,' Malti Aunty mumbled.

'Are they here yet?' Our neighbour, Mrs Murty, asked, sticking her head out of her door.

The lift dinged, the door opened and Cherian, the neighbourhood fish vendor, stepped out with his basket.

'Are they here yet?'

Great. 'Is there anyone in the neighbourhood NOT waiting to meet my group?' I asked Mummy.

'They're here!' the watchman yelled from the main gate. A loud cheer went up along with a smattering of applause. That answered my question.

'Why are there so many people waiting at the gate?' Angry asked. 'Argh, I hate people.'

There had been an even greater ripple of excitement when Danger Cat had stepped out of Chinmay's car and followed him regally to the lift.

'Someone even took a photo of us. I hate photos!'

'Is that Badshah?' someone yelped. 'I swear it is!'

'Ignore them,' I said to Angry. 'Did you bring your flute?'

Angry nodded.

'And Chinmay?'

Chinmay pulled his comb out of his pocket.

‘Fuzzy!’ Dadu beamed. ‘I didn’t know you were in Adi’s group.’

Faizal walked into the room, with my entire family trailing behind him.

‘So tall he’s become!’ Malti Aunty gushed. ‘Eating properly, I tell you. Not like our Adi.’

I watched as Sunny, Mummy and even Malti Aunty exchanged fist bumps with Faizal.

‘We missed you!’ Dadu gushed. ‘Why did you stop coming to play, Fuzzy beta?’

‘Wait, you two know each other?’ Angry asked.

‘I live upstairs,’ Faizal said. ‘Adi and I used to, er, hang out.’

‘Years ago,’ I added. ‘Like, years and years.’

Angry looked curiously from Faizal to me. I could almost hear the gears in her head clicking.

‘You two were friends?’ she asked. Her eyes goggled. Great, one more pair of idli eyes in the house.

‘Not just friends! They were besties,’ Dadu piped up. ‘Chaddi buddies, I tell you!’

‘Dadu! Stop!’ I croaked. Faizal looked just as embarrassed as I felt.

‘Insoupable!’ Sunny nodded. ‘They were deafeningly insoupable.’

I finally managed to get Dadu out of the room, but not before he’d presented us with a dish of jelly, neatly cut into squares.

Chinmay picked up a piece, then dropped it. Danger Cat sniffed the little block, miaowed and leapt to safety.

‘Bro, that jelly just chipped a hole in the floor,’ Angry said, looking closely at the floor.

‘That’s nothing,’ I sighed. ‘His brownies would have gone straight through.’

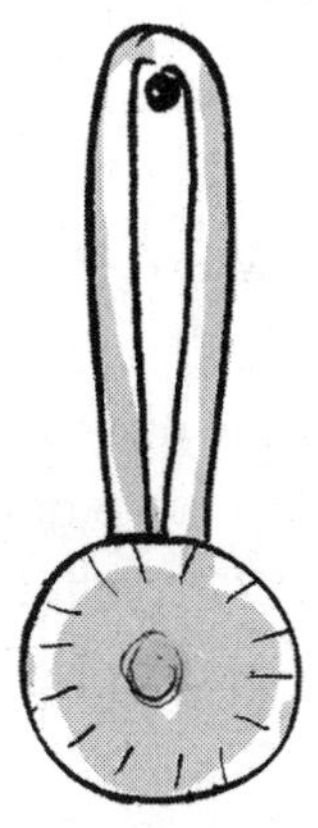

CHAPTER 9
. . . and a Song Is Born!

For the next hour and a half, we worked on our medley. Angry played her line of music over and over and I played bits of songs I thought would work with it. It took a while but we figured out how to fit Chinmay's comb buzzing and Faizal's tambourine jangling in too.

I looked around the room. Faizal and Sunny were doing a jig in one corner. Angry, eating wafers from a snack tray Malti Aunty had brought in, was actually NOT frowning for once. And Chinmay, with Danger Cat perched on his knee, looked so gentle and calm I suddenly wondered why everyone was so scared of him in school. And there it was again—that low hum I'd felt outside the park. That buzz. Something connecting me to this very odd bunch of people—and cat—in my room.

Eh, I was just imagining it, wasn't I?

Almost too soon, it was time to pack up. We heard Chinmay's mom honk the car horn from the gate, and Angry's sister yell, 'AAAANGGRRYYYYYYYY!' I half expected more cheers and clapping, but my neighbours seemed to have gone back home.

'You're good at that,' Angry growled, pointing at my keyboard.

'Uh, thanks,' I said.

'I hate thanks,' she said, but without a frown.

Faizal looked around the room as Angry and Chinmay packed up their stuff. 'You took all your anime posters down,' he said.

'Yeah.'

'And those cute bunny posters as well.'

'You had bunny posters!' Angry snorted.

'I was seven, okay!' I said. 'We all had bunny posters at seven.'

'I still have mine,' Faizal grinned. Then he looked at the wall with all my medals and certificates on it.

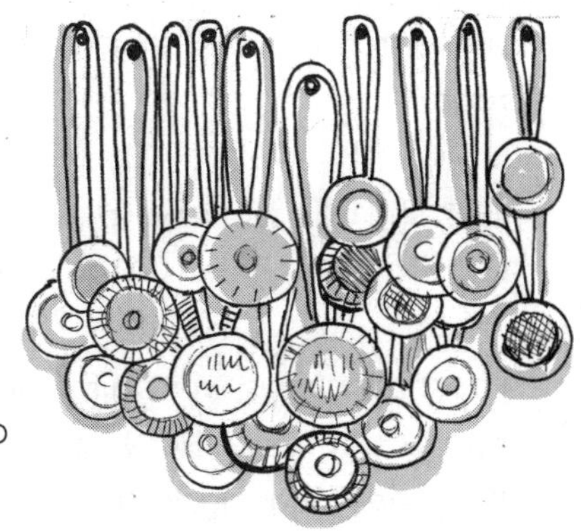

Angry was looking curiously at us again. 'So what happened?'

'Huh?'

'Why did you stop being besties?'

I looked at Faizal. Why *did* we stop being friends? We'd never ever had a fight or anything. We'd just stopped hanging out. And now we were so different I could barely remember how we ever became friends in the first place. Faizal didn't say a thing. He just looked up at my medals, and then at me.

I felt my face go red. But before I could say anything, Dadu knocked on the door.

'Fuzzy beta, look what I found!' he said, waving a framed photograph in the air.

Oh no! Not the photo! 'Dadu, no!'

But Angry was faster. She jumped right up and had the

photograph in her hand before I had even crossed the room.

'Ha!' she said. 'I knew it!' Then she passed the photo to Chinmay.

I closed my eyes, waiting for the laughter and teasing I was sure would follow. But when I opened my eyes, neither of them was laughing. Instead, they peered at the photo and then at me. It was a picture of Faizal and me as seven-year-olds, posing in the most bizarre 70s disco outfits. Our mothers had found us these matching bell-bottoms and shirts, and we had insisted on wearing them every day for months.

'We called them the Disco Duo,' Dadu said proudly. 'They would practise that dance for hours, I tell you!!'

'Show me!' Angry squealed. 'I want to see this dance!'

Faizal beamed. 'Sure! I still know it by heart! Ready, Adi?"

'Erm, I don't remember it,' I lied. 'Okay, bye!'

CHAPTER 10
The Freaky Four

The following week, we performed our song for Miss Meher.

'Wonderful! Wonderful!' she beamed. 'You are a team now!'

'Yes, Miss. But what about the song?' I asked.

'Very interesting!' she said, which is the sort of thing Mummy usually says when Dadu asks her to taste one of his new dishes. 'Keep practising!'

And you know what? We did!

The school had an old keyboard and they let the groups

take turns at it for practice, during breaktime and after school. Angry, Chinmay and Faizal brought their instruments to school. And every day after school, I would practice my part over and over again. Sunny knew it so well he would hum it as he skipped about the house. Dadu began worrying about me spending too much time on 'that little tune'. Even Malti Aunty complained that she had started hearing the tune in her sleep and it was affecting her chapati-making skills.

With each practice session, we were getting better at playing together. Chinmay and Angry had stopped missing their cues, Faizal shook his tambourine at exactly the right spots. And I—well, I found that I had begun to look forward to the bits of group work that weren't about the music. Like when the rest of the group began hanging out at my desk at break time, even when we didn't have practice. Or the time we followed Chinmay out to the far end of the playground where we discovered his secret—a pack of stray cats that he fed every day. And the time Angry scared Kumail away with just a glare after he tried to call us the Weirdo Four. And every now and then, there was that hum, that little buzz.

'We have to have a name, bro,' said Faizal. 'All the other groups have one.'

'We seem to be the Weirdo Four,' Angry frowned. Across the class, Kumail turned to look in our direction, went pale and hurriedly looked away.

'I prefer Freaky Four,' Faizal said. 'Sounds cooler, bro.'

We looked at each other, grinning. Freaky sounded perfect.

This time, when Faizal stuck his fist out, I bumped it right back.

CHAPTER 11

Faizal Throws Some Beats

'There was a fish vendor waiting at the gate to see us,' Angry remarked, as she walked into my room one Saturday. It was the weekend before our Gala, so we had decided to have one last practice session at home.

'That would be Cherian,' I said. 'He missed seeing you earlier.'

'He took a selfie with Danger Cat,' Angry said. 'I hate selfies.'

'Is that monster here too?' Malti Aunty peeked out from behind a bookshelf.

'Who? Mrs Popli?' Dadu looked up from the newspaper, always ready for some gossip.

'That cat!' Malti Aunty hissed. 'That scary beast, that's who.'

'Deafeningly,' I said, as Danger Cat walked in with Chinmay. He was now as much a part of the group as the rest of us, even if he didn't join us at school. At least, I thought he didn't. You never could tell with that Chinmay.

We practised our song, getting it perfectly the first time around. Listen, we had played it so many times by now, we could probably play it in our sleep.

'Once more?' I said. 'Just to be sure.'

Perfect again.

'One last time?' I asked.

Faizal flopped over onto his back across my bed. Angry sank down on the bean bag in the corner. Chinmay looked tired, as he stretched out on the floor with Danger Cat curled up against him. Even Sunny, perched on top of a pile of pillows against the wall, looked sleepy.

'What's wrong, guys?' I asked.

'This song . . . ' Faizal sighed.

'What about it?"

'It's . . . it's just . . . '

'It's what?'

'It's got no Untz, bro,' he said.

'Who-ntz?'

'You know, bro . . . Untz. No beat, no rhythm.'

'Oontz!' Trust Sunny to jump in, waving his hands. 'Oontz! Oontz!'

'It so has!' I snapped. I had worked so hard getting our song just right.

'So doesn't!' Faizal sat up.

'Does!' I felt my face go red.

'Doesn't!'

'Does!' I had practised and practised, I had figured out ways to fit in a stupid comb and a tambourine and that dumb Doe a deer line.

Why was Faizal smiling? And why was he snapping his fingers?

'Doesn't! Doesn't! Does! Doesn't!' he began chanting, as his fingers clicked, his feet tapped, his shoulders twitched. 'Doesn't! Doesn't! Does! Does! Doesn't!'

'Very funny, Faizal,' I said.

But Faizal was now jerking and twitching as he chanted those silly words.

'DOES! DOESN'T! DOES! DOESN'T! VERY FUNNY! DOES! DOESN'T!'

Seriously?

Now Angry was sitting up and her feet were tapping and her fingers were snapping!

'Angry,' Faizal laughed. 'Come on!'

And Angry, looking the least angry I had ever seen her, started chanting, 'Does! Doesn't! Does! Doesn't!'

Faizal's hands flew up to his face. You know what followed. CHAKA CHAKA OOP CHAKA CHAKA CHAKA POW! Faizal danced as he beatboxed, perfectly in time to Angry's words.

Sunny jumped down from his pillow throne, hands high in the air, jumping and squealing with glee.

'Umm, what about practice?' I asked.

And Chinmay was nodding his head, clapping his hands and tapping his feet.

DOES! DOESN'T! DOES! DOESN'T!

WAKAWAKAWAKA UNTZ UNTZ
WAKKA WAKKA WAKKA WOOH!

‘Okay, calm down, guys,’ I tried again.

‘DOES! DOESN’T! DOES! DOESN’T! VERY FUNNY! DOES! DOESN’T!’

KIKIKIKI WOMP WOMP TAKATAKA POW!

With one final KAPOW and one last squeal, the four of them collapsed on the floor, laughing.

It was crazy. It was ridiculous. It was.

‘Guys, get serious,’ I said.

‘Oh yeah? How come you’re smiling then?’ Angry said, peering up at me from the floor.

‘I hate smiling,’ I said, and watched them fall over giggling, again.

CHAPTER 12

Crocodiles, Radishes . . . and a Gala

'Ready?' Miss Meher asked.

'Ready, Miss,' Class 5C yelled. It was Friday—the day of the Gala!

I stood with the rest of my class in the big green room beside the auditorium. In ten minutes, it would be the Freaky Four's turn to get up on stage before all the Grade 5 parents and perform our medley. I walked over to where Faizal stood by the window, tapping his foot to some tune only he could hear.

'I don't get it,' I said.

'Huh?'

'Why did you let me pick the song for the gala? Why didn't you suggest burpboxing?'

'Hey!'

'Okay, beatboxing. But you know what I mean.'

Faizal shrugged. 'Miss Meher would probably have said no.'

'Not I if she'd heard you err, throw beats,' I said. 'You are pretty good.'

'You think so?"

I nodded. 'You know you are, Faizal.'

For a long moment, Faizal said nothing. Then, softly, he said, 'Crocodiles.'

'Huh?'

'Crocodiles,' he said again. 'I know you hate being in groups. And how much you like winning.'

'We are not going to win anything today,' I said.

'Are you sure? Because I heard Miss Meher telling the

principal we sounded really good, and different from the other groups. And that she was really looking forward to our performance today. Kumail said even Risha was looking a little grumpy after hearing you practise last week.'

'Seriously?' I felt my heart start thudding harder, like one of those dishes falling down the stairs in Faizal's beats. Maybe I could still grab a medal out of the crocodile's jaws. 'Wait, you said "Risha".'

'Ya, bro. Didn't you see the noticeboard? She changed her name back to the original one. Feels weird saying it now, without extra Hs and Is and . . .

'Radishes!' we both said together, and laughed.

And in the din of the room, with all my classmates chattering and dragging chairs around, I felt it again—that little buzz, that zing.

'What about the Untz, though?' I asked. 'You said we didn't have it.'

Faizal shrugged again.

I looked across the room at Angry and Chinmay, sitting quietly in the far corner. Angry had her frown on as usual, but for a moment I remembered her singing and dancing and laughing in my room during our practice session. Chinmay had seemed different too, as he'd clapped alone.

'Adi, Faizal, your group is next,' Miss Meher announced.

We walked up and took our positions. I could feel my hands trembling. Strange, I thought. Because my hands never trembled. After all my hours of practice, my fingers knew their way around the keys. I stared down into the audience, spotting Papa, Mummy and Dadu, with Sunny right by the central aisle.

'And we now present Group 6—Adi, Angira, Chinmay and Faizal,' Miss Meher was saying.

This was it, I thought, as I sat down before the keyboard set up on stage. Beside me, Chinmay, Angry and Faizal were at the microphones assigned to them. In a moment, I would play the opening bars of our medley and, one by one, the rest of the group would join in. And, in exactly five minutes, we would be done, and I would be free of the crocodile.

Except, I couldn't.

I looked down at my hands and suddenly, they felt like the hands of a stranger.

I just sat there, looking at the keys.

'Children, you can begin,' Miss Meher said from the wings. She waved her hands, urging us to start.

I turned to look at Faizal, Angry and Chinmay. They nodded, waiting for me to begin.

Then I leaned into the mic and yelled.

CHAPTER 13
The Untz!

'CHILLAX YO' CHILLLLLL!'

Everyone in the auditorium froze!

I turned to Faizal, half expecting to see him grin and say something about the Untz.

He was frozen too. He clutched his tambourine, his eyes giant dosas of horror.

You know how in the books someone always sees their whole life rush before their eyes when something terrifying is about to happen?

Well, my life did just that. It flipped and bipped like those old-time movie reels people watched back when dinosaurs roamed in the football field. Then it zoomed, like an army of cats, right before my eyes. A mad rush of Fuzzy and me, and Dadu and Sunny, and dancing and keyboard playing in an empty room. I saw medals (whoa!) and Risha (yuck!). I saw Angry hanging from a tree and Chinmay humming to his cats and even Danger Cat glaring at me. And suddenly, I knew what that little buzz was.

The Untz, the beat, the happy rhythm that bound us all, and made us friends, made us the Freaky Four.

I looked straight into the audience and said, even louder than before—

Faizal was still frozen. Angry stood with her mouth open. Chinmay, beside her, might as well have been a statue of himself.

'UNTZ! UNTZ! UNTZ!' I sang, waving my hands the way I'd seen Fuzzy do. 'Come on, Fuzzy! UNTZ! UNTZ! UNTZ!'

Fuzzy didn't move.

What had I done? I had messed it all up, ruined all the work we'd put in!

A low murmur arose from the audience. Any moment now, Miss Meher was going to appear and drag us all off stage. Principal Vichare would give me one of his long lectures. And Risha, with no extra H's, I's or rhinoceroses, would tease me about it till the end of time.

Which is when the miracle happened.

OONS! OONS!

'OONS! OONS! OONS!' a high thin voice sang out from the audience. I saw Faizal look up, startled, then smile.

'OONS! OOONS! OONS!' The voice rang out again through the dark hall. I would know my little brother's voice anywhere. And a lilt, a beat in his voice told me . . . he felt the Untz too.

'UNTZ! UNTZ! UNTZ!' I sang, along with my little brother.

And as we threw down our beats, Sunny and I, someone else joined in.

'REHAAAAAAAAAAAAN!' Angry's voice rang out, perfectly in time with us. Angry, who hated the flute and the stage and singing and mics and the dark. And as she turned and smiled at me across the stage, I knew she'd caught the Untz too.

'WHO IS REHAAN? WHO IS REHAAN?' Angry and I shouted together. 'WHO IS REHAAN? WHO IS REHAAN?'

A couple of boys in the audience stood up, confused. Clearly, we had some Rehaans watching.

Chinmay started clapping along, and snapping his fingers. And at just the right moment, he began humming in tune to our crazy song.

‘WHO IS REHAAN? WHO IS REHAAN?’ we sang, clapping our hands, snapping our fingers, humming. And as we clapped and snapped and hummed—and Sunny bounced about the aisle, still singing ‘OONS! OONS! OONS!’ . . . well, finally, finally Faizal came to life!

‘DOOOOO! CHEWY CHEWY CHEWY CHEWY!’

The audience gasped, then giggled. But a few hands began clapping too, and I could see heads nodding and shoulders twitching in time to our strange song.

‘TOK TOK TOKK! TAKKA TAKKA TOK TOK TOKK . . . FREAKYYYYYYY FOURRRRR!’

Now Fuzzy stepped into the beat, made it his own and threw it right back to the crowd. Angry and I stepped back. We stood there, our feet tapping, our heads nodding, in time to his beats. And we grinned like monkeys, out at the audience and at each other. Down at the foot of the stage, Sunny was dancing, jumping, shaking with so much joy a couple of other kids jumped up to join him.

Was it great music? Nope.

Was it a medal-winning sonata? Nu-uh.

But it was a beat that we felt together, and that made all the difference.

And Chinmay's tuneless humming probably had an Untz all its own, because it brought the cats back.

MRAAAOOOOWR!

RAAARGH!

MEOOOOOOWR!

The audience gasped, then tittered as Danger Cat appeared out of the shadows, purring loudly. Behind him came an army of cats, all mewing and purring and yowling. Chinmay, without missing a beat, bent down and picked Danger Cat up and held him up to the mic. And as Faizal threw out his beats and Chinmay hummed, Danger Cat and his army sang along.

'My baby!' someone screamed in the audience. 'That's my Badshah!' Mrs Popli, mother of pests, speller of names to ward off evil eyes, stood up in the audience. And as Danger Cat rumbled into the mic, she began clapping along.
It was chaos. It was ridiculous.

It was wonderful.

One by one, the audience picked up the clapping.

'Fuzzy!' I said. 'Now!'

And I ran out into the centre of the stage and struck a pose. A pose I'd last made as a seven-year-old in a grainy photograph with my bestie.

For one long moment, Faizal stared at me.

And then the auditorium and the crowd and even all the noise seemed to fade away and it was just Fuzzy and me—the Disco Duo.

CHAPTER 14
All Kinds of Medals

'I don't get it.' It was RishaWishaQuisha lurking out in the corridor by the water cooler. The gala had ended, and we were packing up to head home.

'You guys practised so hard. You were actually . . . ' She waggled her hand in the air.

'Good?' I suggested. 'Excellent? Amazing?'

'I was going to say "almost in tune",' she sniffed.

'We weren't going to win, though.'

'Ya, true. We were really good.' She shrugged. 'But bro, you guys didn't even try. And what was that dance you and Faizal performed! I don't think I've ever laughed so much in my life.'

I grinned. It had been ridiculous. But also amazing. For all the laughs we had got, there were cheers and loud claps too. And as Miss Meher had finally led us off stage, kids had giggled and pointed, but some also gave us fist bumps and high fives.

'Ya, whatever, Fisha,' I said. 'Sometimes it's not about the medal. And congrats on winning, by the way.'

Risha gasped. 'Who are you and what have you done with that annoying pest Adi?'

'Now spell that with three Hs and a sausage,' I laughed.

She rolled her eyes. 'I've told my mom she has to stop with the spellings,' she said. 'Or I'm going to run away, like Badshah.'

‘You’ll always be A-N-N-O-Y-I-N-G to me.’

‘Haha, takes one to know one,’ she grinned. ‘So if it’s not always about the medals, does this mean you won’t take part in the Quiz? Or the Olympiad? Or the Spelling Bee?’

I stopped. I hadn’t thought about anything but the gala for the last six weeks.

‘Seriously?’ Risha stared at me. ‘You’re, like, retiring from medals?’

‘Umm,’ I said.

‘Because, bro,’ she shrugged. ‘It’s no fun winning medals alone.’

Oh! All this time, all this fighting and scrabbling for medals with Risha—well, that had been OUR beat, the rhythm that kept us going, from one quiz and gala and bee to the next. The medals, sure, but also the fun of battling each other.

‘Did you just say “This is our Untz”?’ Risha said.

I really had to stop mumbling. ‘Ugh. You wish,’ I lied, heading down the corridor to where my family waited for me.

‘Bro, YOU WISH I wish!’ Risha laughed, just as the door swung shut behind me.

***

Who am I, though? And what have I done with Adi?

Listen, I still love medals, okay? And winning. I still like being good at the keyboard and even better at maths. I know I'm going to be hanging out with Angry and Chinmay and Faizal and, who knows, even Danger Cat. And I will also join that advanced maths class I begged Mummy for. After all, I'd hate to leave poor Risha to win all those medals without a fight.

There are all kinds of rhythms in me, lots of burps and crashing dishes and buzzing combs that add up to the beat I throw down. I can be sonata and KAPOW, Disco Duo and Freaky Four. I can, like Risha, spell myself any old way I want. It's all part of the Untz of me!

And guess what, all of these feel like medals too.

And if this makes you roll your eyes and wonder what's wrong with me? Well . . .

Chillax yo' chill, bro.

Just blame it on the Untz.

ACKNOWLEDGEMENTS

Aparna, my editor, for making me a Power POFFS girl, and for getting the unruly chords of this story playing in harmony

Bijal, for listening to this song, and for feeling the Untz

ABOUT THE AUTHOR AND ILLUSTRATOR

Lavanya Karthik is a writer, illustrator and award-winning nap taker. Her naps have taken her across the world where she has had many adventures as a ninja, an evil mastermind and a shark whisperer. When she is awake, she can be found in Mumbai, planning her next nap.